ANCHOR BOOKS

SIXTY SOMETHING

Edited by

David Foskett

Foreword

Anchor Books is a small press, established in 1992, with the aim of promoting readable poetry to as wide an audience as possible.

We hope to establish an outlet for writers of poetry who may have struggled to see their work in print.

The poems presented here have been selected from many entries. Editing proved to be a difficult and daunting task and as the Editor, the final selection was mine.

The poems chosen represent a cross-section of styles and content. They have been sent from all over the world, written by young and old alike, united in the passion for writing poetry.

I trust this selection will delight and please the authors and all those who enjoy reading poetry.

David Foskett
Editor

CONTENTS

TRAPPED

When I first went to School at the age of five
I slowly came to realise
I had to sit for hours on end
I found it difficult to comprehend
It dawned on me I was no longer free
To run about and play with glee
When I left School it was even worse
Going to work with remorse
Holidays became a thing of the past
Working at Christmas right up to the last
When I got married I thought I'd be free
Running a home and being just me
None of my time was really my own
I could never get *'space'* and time alone
Alas! I had done an awful mishap
Falling into the marital trap
I was in charge, in a kind of way
Deciding how I would spend the day
With children around in demand
Not always obeying every command
At last the young ones flew the nest
The time I thought would be the best
But life took its toll
I started to ail
Arthritis and ailments making me frail
My husband took ill and passed away
Leaving me alone all day
I am *sixty-plus* and trying to cope
Struggling on, it is really no joke
Now I am free to go where I please
I am trapped in the house
With my Arthritic knees!

Evelyn A Evans

SIXTY SOMETHING

Sixty took me by surprise
I felt its approach but closed my eyes.
What day, what year did youth forsake me
Did time unseen just overtake me?
The change in me seemed to occur
When shop assistants called me sir,
Young women smiled at me for I rather
Reminded them of their dear old father.
Sixty something's fine for some
For they can jog and they can run.
Some swim in winter full of zest
While I shrink inside my woollen vest,
My fingers go all numb and white
I need more bed clothes on at night.
I need more time to cross the road
When carrying out the green cross code
During summer I seek the shade
For in the sun I tend to fade.
When I think about my state pension
It's enough to give me hypertension,
I don't mean to make a fuss
Just because I'm sixty plus
But now I find I have more time
To congregate my thoughts in rhyme.

Richard F Youngs

THE FLEETING YEARS

There's an old lady lives down our street,
Rather eccentric but awfully sweet,
Fiercely independent, always polite,
Some people say she's not quite right,
Because she views the world in a different light
Always the optimist, thinks the best hasn't arrived,
Quietly determined to get on with her life,
Helping old people across the road,
Giving up my seat on a bus,
Helping to carry their heavy load,
It's so sad to grow old,
I glance at my reflection in the looking glass,
There's an old lady looking back at me,
The one I never see.

J Burton Taylor

A TUMULUS TOO FAR?

For the third time,
I sit in tumulus ring,
And think, as twice before,
Of those ancient men,
Who bore their chieftain's corpse,
Up here to bury him.
This is a wild place,
With long eyed views, he will not see again.
Nor me, perhaps, for five miles, in and out,
Across fell and limestone pavement,
Is a longish way alone, at sixty-six.

Yet I'm glad I've come,
The odd three thousand years,
Since he was brought, and I have walked,
Are but a blink of eternity's eye,
And up here, with rocks and grass,
Stunted trees and mountains round,
The scene today is much the same,
As his mourning friends,
Looked out upon,
Before they left him, neatly laid,
And covered with the stones.

The clouds still roll in from the west,
The wind still sharp and keen.
Nothing moves except my pen,
And he has not,
For these three thousand years.
He knew not Christ, as I,
But did he worship here,
As I do, now?

Roger Hodges

4

RETIREMENT

Time to think of days gone by
To sit and watch the birds on high
Gaze up to a clear blue sky

Time to sit and meditate
For leaning on the garden gate
Gently dream and appreciate

Time to live and take delight
In the radiant sun so bright
Enjoy the tranquil of the night

Time to take up new pursuits
Find the one that really suits
Travel around by different routes

Time to do so many things
Enjoy each day the morning brings
This is what retirement brings

Time to value most of all
The hand of friendship from one and all
Cherished ever, to oft recall
Time.

Madeleine Robins

THE PROS AND CONS OF REACHING SIXTY

To gain experience and confidence
Over storm ridden years
Wiser now and stronger
To face enemies and fears
To travel on a ticket
Saving pounds from visits
To places long forgotten
That we used to frequent
often.
When we were young.

But how I miss
That unexpected kiss
On a crowded thoroughfare
That only the young can savour
Without a care
Not for the over sixties
To embrace like this
It would just make passers by
Stop and stare

S M Cox

6

SIXTY SOMETHING

Yes I am sixty something
But I'm going to keep you guessing,
It *is* a woman's privilege
And it's really quite a blessing
To pretend you're younger than you are
It's so good for the morale,
So now you know the writer
Is really quite a gal.
I'm passed what they call retirement
And it really is quite fun
Going daily round the town
Taking stock of everyone,
Chatting to odd passers-by
And of course I must confess,
I do appreciate the young
And the modern way they dress.
I find them quite refreshing
In their conversation too
And it's lovely to be listening
To the youngsters' point of view,
Sixty something ain't so bad
It's good to be alive,
Yes I'm fifteen over sixty
I'm a ripe old seventy five.

Mary Skelton

WE AIN'T DEAD YET

I always thought with age would come
A wise and tolerant me,
Instead I get more tetchy
With all the family.
They expect me to be gracious
Placid and content,
Like a granny ought to be
To smell of lilac scent.
To hell with that, I still want fun
I feel I'm in my prime,
My hormones haven't yet expired
I'm not on borrowed time.
I've done my duty by the kids
The old man's up and left,
Now I'm living just for me,
You ain't seen nothing yet.
Grannies of the world unite
We'll show them how it's done,
Kick your heels up one more time
Life ain't just for the young

Margaret Malenoir

REFLECTION

In a few weeks time I will be sixty: pass from middle to old age:
An OAP, an appendage of the State.
Will I greet my kismet calmly, or lash out in futile rage
Regretting undone things now it's too late?

I've never entered politics or written any books;
My home's not featured in posh magazines:
No-one envies me my lifestyle or wants to have my looks;
I'm not one of the world's brave heroines.

I dearly would have liked to find that touch of fragile fame;
To leave a part of me to recall:
But, as it is, when I am gone, no-one will know my name;
No monument to show I've lived at all.

So now approaching sixty, I can look back on my life;
A nobody who never made the grade;
An ordinary daughter, mother, grandmother and wife
Drifting through each subsequent decade.

But now a whole new world is poised to open up for me:
Life takes on new meaning once again.
Fresh doors to unlock, the pension book provides the key.
So pop the cork and open the champagne!

June Steele

PROGRESS

I do not feel old until I tell of my youth
And innocent eyes make me long in the tooth
Of bathtime in kitchen in long metal tub
With water warmed up from coal burning hub
No carpets on floors but lino all shiny
And hand woven rag rug in bedroom so tidy
The freezing cold house apart from one fire
To be warm back and front was my desire

When a car was a new thing that came down the street
And neighbours spent ages at gate post to meet
When sweets were not wrapped but stuck in the paper
And barrels held biscuits and little green caper
The pavements and road drains the housewife would clean
So her house frontage like the neighbours would gleam
Front door steps were whitened with water and stone
Whether family or single you were never alone

When things taken for granted in this modern age
Meant scrimping and saving to earn extra wage
Not for a holiday or luxury sweet
But so that the family had shoes on their feet
Now neighbours close doors and build fences high
And enquiring is nosy and worrying to pry
The noise of community no longer is *nice*
No wonder society is paying the price.

Jane Darnell

LOOKING FORWARD

Oh the big sixty with all its fears
I'm female such a blessing
to have to wait five more years
would have been so frustrating

I pray I'll still have good health
When I retire to leisure
I know I won't have much wealth
but retiring will be a pleasure

Maureen Dawson

OLD BONES FROM YOUNG BLOOD

My name these days is old bones and their pain
Not the age that made them turned them to chalk
Through the three score years and more I now gain
That gave me leave to live to breathe to walk
Through the first fire of youth's wild passion
From a bawling babe whose first blood red breath
Led me into life once there to fashion
Me into this that I am now near death
O that blood that once when I was but young
Coursed through me rich pumped by an ardent heart
As rich as any song was ever sung
And learned before all blood and bones depart
Young blood to old bones turns should time allow
As ages pass to ages I pass now

W J T

SIXTY PLUS

I was born between two brothers,
Copied everything they did
So I climbed walls and trellises
When I was just a kid.
My days were so exciting,
There was such a lot to do.
But what I did not realise
That time was passing too,
So, comes the day, I cannot bend,
I find it hard to kneel.
And when I sit in my armchair,
It's always tired I feel.
There is no cause to worry
It comes to all of us.
A complaint that's known as growing old
Which means you're sixty plus.
But now I've reached the eighty plus
My husband - ninety plus,
Though we've been wed over sixty years
There is still the two of us.

Lillian J Lucas

SIXTY PLUS

Life was good, and a lot of fun
When you got the key at twenty one,
A little bit thrifty, you're more
Thoughtful by the time you're thirty.

Middle age spread can be costly
Who said 'Life begins at forty'?
It's busy, busy and all go, go
Approaching is the big five O.

Aches and pains are not so nifty
They're all there by the time you're sixty
Armed with bus pass for all to see
Teeth and glasses, you're an OAP.
No more work (for which you're paid)
Here's good health for the next decade.

P Robertson

SIXTY SOMETHING

Granny's off her rocker
The family all agree,
She doesn't knit,
or baby sit.
So wherever can she be?

Now granny's off her rocker
All the family gather round.
An unpaid Nan.
was not the plan,
Now she's nowhere to be found.

'Is granny off her rocker?'
Say the family in dispute
Gone to the Gym.
Just to slim.
Her ailment is acute.'

Yes, granny's off her rocker
and now she's off to town.
Looking cute
in knee length suit.
There's no holding granny down.

Gran's rocking chair is idle.
The kitchen quietly strange
To start anew.
At sixty two
Is now living for a change.

A B Chabaluk

PATIENCE

When I was young time went so slow I really couldn't wait
For school days to be over and get out of that gate,
I never wanted to go to bed, bedtime came too soon,
I wished that was the sun up there instead it was the moon,
Never ending seconds waiting for the clock to chime
To say that it's Christmas Day, *now* it's opening presents time,
My mother used to tell me not to wish my time away
For time is very precious and I'd understand one day,
I wanted to grow up and have make-up on my face,
I wanted grown up dresses made of satin and of lace,
I dreamed of Mr Wonderful who often gave me a glance
But then I'd play the wallflower when he asked someone else to dance,
I wanted to have a husband and have children too,
Then to have grandchildren, there was so much to do,
'If only I were older', I always used to say,
Never realising that soon would come the day
That I would be a pensioner, sixtyish I'm aghast,
Now I know without being told that time just goes so fast,
So now that I am older and retired I have become,
Most of my young wishes already have been done,
I ponder on my memories and sit and reminisce,
I don't have to rush these days and that to me is bliss,
Time for others, time for myself, why couldn't this always be?
But it's not 'till you get older that you begin to see,
That patience is a virtue, believe that as you may,
Take the time to live your life and treasure every day.

Elaine Spalding

GROWING OLD GRACEFULLY

They say at *'forty'* we are *'over the hill'*
But I believe we are *'with it'* still,
Our wrinkles are hardly showing,
Most of us still slim and neat.
With luck we are still glowing,
Our faces fresh and figures petite.
But sixty is a different *'Kettle of Fish'*
No longer are we considered some *'dish'*
Just a little one's granny.
Our ego gone, our eyesight amiss,
We rarely, if ever, receive a kiss,
Our pleasures now are simple,
But we are truly blessed,
A baby's little dimple,
Will give us happiness.
And though we walk, instead of run,
Life is still so much fun.

Dorothy King

60 PLUS - GETTING OLD

Can you forget your robust past?
No thought then it could not last.
Of course you should have been aware
must pass the days of do and dare.

O youth you curtain raiser of life's play,
seldom does the limelight bright,
confirm you've got your act just right.
Applause not often comes your way.

But time goes on, you're getting greyer.
it seems you are the last to know
that waiting in the wings that immortal slayer
where his scythe points to your final show.

You remember times you fell from grace
but growing wiser as you got older
your conscience wagged its finger in your face
and you take heed, you take your days less bolder.

Time still goes on, you forget past struggles and strife
you remember that unforgettable girl
Who set your mind a-whirl,
The day she said she'd be your wife.

Children came, took jam from your bread,
could not pay with money, but as a better spread,
brought their own brand of honey,
sweetness that will last for all the days ahead.

Arthur Romero

SIXTY SOMETHING

The days are short, the nights get cold,
And I am feeling, Oh! So old.
When I awake and rise from bed,
After laying down my sleepy head.
Another day has just begun,
Hopefully filled with far more fun,
As I grow old, and youth passes by,
I stop to think, I've changed and why.
Each day gets harder, as I grow weak,
I feel more hopeless and far more meek.
By dinner time, my aches have gone,
I feel much better, and far more strong.
As day comes round, and teatime gets nearer,
My aches comes back and life is clearer.
I'm getting older, and far less fit,
My mind is going, along with my wit.
As I climb the stairs, to my bedroom door,
I know sleep is needed, but I'm not so sure.
Laying in my comfy bed,
Once more, I rest my sleepy head,
Feeling cold, and body like lead.
I shut my eyes and go to sleep,
Knowing tomorrow,
Will have to damn well keep

Les Croft

SIXTY PLUS

I'm sixty plus and by the way,
I'm feeling younger every day,
No longer have to watch the time,
Just sit right down and write in rhyme,
OK there is lots to do.
Cleaning up and gardening too,
My grandson comes down for a day,
That's when there are games to play,
I watch the soaps enjoy the lot,
And TV quizzes miss them not,
Every day flies by so fast,
Good job my working days are past.

Kathleen Egan

DO I CRY FOR MY YOUTH

Do I cry for my youth again
For the years that have gone?
Or do I look with disdain
At the memories I lean upon?

Do I cry to be forever young
For youth's impetuosity?
To relive the feelings I had flung
From my mind to save my sanity?

Do I want the cycle to start
Once more for me to see
That if I could take my life apart
Would I have lived it differently?

Do I long for my youth once more
To see if I would gain
The chance to even every score
Of whatever caused me pain?

Would I change this cloak of bliss
For youth's trial and error?
Oh no! I cannot dismiss
This happy face reflecting in my mirror.

Jean M Shansky

SIXTY SOMETHING

What is sixty something!
Sweet words of youth
Have passed him by.
Where has that certain glint gone
Which shone from his eyes,
The sparkle of love
No longer there.

There he sits
In that chair,
Book in hand
No words to say.
How do I find
My loved one
Who went away.

If only time stood still
I would pick a certain year.
My love one so youthful
A lover - one so dear.
One I thought
I would have
Year after year.

Where did he go
In his sixty fifth year.
How I wish,
He would recall
The thrill of love
Magic
He offered to all.

Margaret J Franklin

SIXTY SOMETHING

Sixty seems so far away, I feel so very *'young'*,
Although I'm only fifty-six I feel as I have sprung
From babe in arms beside the fire -
To grandmama with hair turned white? - Not quite!
Looking forward to retirement? I should say I am
Many years I've worked, to earn my bread and jam
It's very true what *'they'* say -
There's just never enough hours in one day.
There's lots of things I want to do, I shall not
be bored - I'm telling you! - Poetry, gardening,
Drawing too, and my grandchildren, to name but a few,
of things stored up inside my head, been there a long time
but never dead.
I have never had much in the way of wealth
But more important I have had good health
I hope that will remain for the next four years
I might even shed a few tears?
Sixty something you say? I say - you are as young
as you want to be - Roll on, the next few years.

Doreen Brooks

SIXTY SOMETHING

At sixty, we can have such fun
Dance all night when day is done.
So get your dance shoes out again.
I've booked the coach, we're off to Spain
We're old enough to know, for sure.
The things we want, can't ask for more.
Yet young enough to get them done.
This time, the road leads to the sun.
We can ride a bus and train half-fare,
Stay out late and no-one to care.
Lovely, we can please ourself,
Leave our troubles on the shelf.
We can stay up late again.
Or we can go to bed by ten.
In our lovely cottage, with a view.
We have more to learn, and lots to do.
Study art, just for art's sake.
Paint a mountain or a lake.
Write a poem of life's way
Recall the fun and happy days.
And time to do the many things
That being sixty something brings.

Gwladys Gahan

SIXTY PLUS

I was looking forward and about to retire
    Thinking how nice to be lazy and sit by the fire.
Do what one likes and not have to work,
    Put aside jobs I'd like to shirk.

But now I have found things much more fun
    Than working all week till day is done.
I joined a group and learnt many crafts.
    And we have shows of foreign parts.

We go on outings. Our world is much wider.
    And holidays too, now we know each other.
My work used to keep me from booking a hol.
    Now many brochures their bounties extol

But what is so nice is to renew old friends
    To find friendship sweeter as life extends.
Did I think I would sit here to just grow old?
    Life has so many interests as the years unfold.

Margaret Gaines

IN MY SIXTIES

I think it bold, to say I'm old,
Now that I'm in my sixties.
No need to rush, what's all the fuss,
I still sew a fine seam, have the time to dream,
I can eat lovely cream cakes for my tea,
Now that I'm in my sixties.

To tell the truth I still love to dance,
At today's pop tunes, as I did in my youth,
In my garden, I plant flowers,
I love to read for hours,
Now that I'm in my sixties.

In summer I walk my dog, as I do in winter's fog,
And for my ills, the doctor gives me pills,
Although my eyes are getting dim,
But in my new eye-glasses, I can now see my lashes,
And if my hair needs a trim,
I'm not so old, and I won't be told,
Now that I'm in my sixties.

You can never grow old, so I've been told,
When there is poetry in your heart.

Joan McAvoy

26

IF WE HAD KNOWN

Old age, how can we atone, for wrinkled
skin and fragile bone,
Once so young and very strong,
Not knowing in youth, we were doing such   wrong.
Sun made our skin that was once so fair,
Very dark brown, but we did not care.
All we knew it was the trend,
To have a tan without an end.

Smoking, that was another fad
Then, it was not known to be bad.
We wish we had not dyed our hair,
As now it is showing some wear and tear.

Our teeth, also we never knew,
All the modern things to do,
To bite now, we hesitate,
Always afraid we will break our plate.

We may have saved ourselves some pain
If we had not been so very vain,
Winkle picker shoes, the fashion
Our feet were pinching, our faces ashen,
But in our youth would we have thought?
That bunions came with the shoes we bought.

Now looking back on those carefree days,
Would we really have changed our ways?
No, for if our lives could start again.
We would *still* be suffering all of the pain.

Carol Shaikh

RETIREMENT

Sixty years
And now, what next?

Relaxation - had
Enough of stress,
Time to dream,
Idleness,
Recreation,
Education,
Memories,
Expectation.
New experiences
Trepidation?

Margaret E Turtle

RETIREMENT

Eighteen months then I shall be free
To do what I like, to please only me
To lay in my bed *'til ten in the morn'*
Or get up and hear the birds sing in the dawn.

I'll have my bus pass and train ticket too
I can ride free from here to waterloo
Travel around London on sight-seeing tours
And marvel at things I've never seen before.
I'll go with a friend to a theatre or two
Ice shows and musicals, there's plenty to do
Or just feed the pigeons in Trafalgar Square
And chat to the tourists without any care.
I'll sit by the lake in St James' Park
Or listen to the band and leave before dark.

Maybe I'll catch a coach to the sea
Fares are reduced for a pensioner like me
I'll take a packed lunch and tea in a flask
And sit back in comfort and watch the country go past.
Or maybe I'll ask a friend on a tour
To some far off place we haven't been to before
We'll just take things easy and have a good chat
We won't have to worry about what time we'll get back
And when I retire you'll be hearing me say,
There's so much to do and not enough time in the day.

S Pickrell

MY RETIREMENT ROOM

One day soon I'll be sixty five
So I'll retire on that day,
It's then I'll enter God's Waiting Room
For, I hope, a very long stay.

I know it will be a happy room
For to Heaven is the only way out,
And everyone enters at some time
That's what life is all about,
I'll be happy in God's Waiting Room
Making the most of each day,
Until I hear His call to 'Come in'
Which will be many years hence, I pray.

One could say that one's whole life on earth
Is God's Waiting Room for mankind,
But I like to think when I retire
In God's Waiting Room, pleasure I'll find.

So everyone who is living on earth
Should make the most of each day,
For, in some way, we're all in God's Waiting Room
Until His voice says 'Come, Heaven's this way'.

Harry Ireland

AGE

The age of innocence has passed
Your youth now part of your past
A child until the end, until the last
But your fate was certain, the runes were cast

Growing wiser, growing older
Greying hairs, getting colder
Living with a chip upon your shoulder
Getting braver, getting bolder

And as you try to regain your childhood
Your age becomes a falsehood

Christopher Marsden

RETIREMENT

Retirement is not waking early,
Retirement is going to bed late.
Retirement is owning a diary,
In order to check on the date.
Retirement is less work and more play
With a pension replacing your pay.
Retirement is this life's reward,
For the work goals you have scored.

Pamela R Pickford

SIXTY SOMETHING

She closed her eyes
What a story to be told
Of bygone days, now she'd grown old
Those tired old fingers once nimble and quick
Now carefully cradled her walking stick
Only memories are left in this tired old frame
Of busy vibrant days, locked away to remain
Just a memory, a fleeting pretence
Gone for ever, but with her to remain
To lighten the dark days, once again.

Irene Pearce

SIXTY SOMETHING

To listen to the pouring rain
While I sit by the fire
Oh I can't wait to be sixty
How I would love to retire

To wake up in the morning
And plan my whole day through
Instead of rushing down the road
To catch the eight o' two

I would like to take a holiday
I have not been for years
To sit and watch the changing tide
Or take a stroll along the pier

I don't want good fortune
Nor do I crave for wealth
I just want to retire
And live life in good health

Gillian Morrisey

YOUR TOOTH'S TOO LONG

Some wise pundit in his patter
Stated this obvious truth,
'If you don't mind, it don't matter,
When comparing age with youth'.

But is it just a quirk of fate
That she was born far too late?
And I, a balding, portly loon,
Was born alas, far too soon.
And an old man, wedding a young girl
Is surely round the bend,
For aping those who simply buy
Books to be read by a friend?

Sam Stafford

ENJOYING RETIREMENT

We thought retirement would be great.
To lounge around we couldn't wait.
A game of golf with some friends.
But this is where the fun time ends.

The phone is ringing it's the school.
We had to call it is the rule.
Your grand-daughter is feeling sick.
Can you get here very quick.

Dearest Dad we have a lapse
In bath routine, we've broke the taps.
Of we go to Do-it-Yourself.
The taps are over on that shelf.

Next it's Mother feeling ill.
Can you come and get my pill.
She's quite all right I can see.
She only wants to talk to me.

Son has broken window pane.
Board is keeping out the rain.
Can you call and get the glass.
If by chance the shop you pass.

Mother-in-law decides to move.
That we are fit we have to prove.
Moving boxes large and small.
We know now we're not fit at all.

Shopping, moving, doing odd jobs.
Baby sitting what's the odds.
Our duties we do not shirk.
How did we find time to go to work.

Pat Lambourne

GERIATRICS

They call us *'geriatrics'* when we're 65,
I don't mind, my skin is thick, I'm glad to be alive,
No-one can stop at 21, however much we'd like,
We all grow old, let's face it, so come on, on your trike.

Come and join our *'pop'* group,
You could have lots of fun,
We're called *'Gerry and the 'at tricks'*,
We play till day is done.

Life is short, let's live it!
We can't afford to wait,
With new hip joints and some repairs,
It could improve our gait!

We might live till we're 99,
Now that would be a sin,
The powers that be would have a fit,
And put us in the bin.

What short memories folk have got,
We helped to win the war,
But then that was an age ago,
It doesn't count no more.

Audrey Pincombe

RETIREMENT?

Although I'm growing older, for the years are passing by
I cannot think of myself as 'old' no matter how I try.
I know I've lots of grey hairs and my skin is wrinkling too,
But I have to keep active for there still is much to do.

Days just don't seem long enough for all the things I plan,
My housework I'll relinquish when my thoughts begin to scan.
I'll just have to read the books still on my shelves, unread,
And write so many letters before I go to bed.

I listen to the radio and all my records, too,
As music from my teenage years comes back to me anew.
I'd like to take up riding and learn the proper way to swim,
And write a famous novel, before my mind grows dim.

To go walking in green meadows, upon hills mid woodland trees,
Or sail upon the ocean, or learn to master skis.
I'd like to go Ballooning, I mean the hot air kind,
Such a wonderful way-to-view the countryside.
And then of course there's Concorde I've yet to travel by
So many places still to see across those miles of sky.

Kids call me 'Recycled Teenager' (although I am a Gran)
I don't believe they are all bad, so I'll help them if I can.
I hope I keep quite healthy to do some of these things,
There was insufficient time before, but now *'Retirement'* brings.

Joan Heybourn

THE MIRROR

She looks and thinks who can that be?
I know it surely can't be me,
The wrinkles and the lines I see,
Just simply don't belong to me,
The sagging chin is there to see,
She bends her head and there are three,
But though I'm sixty plus I'm great.
I know I look just twenty eight!

Patricia Watling

BEING OLD

Being old is much more fun,
You have more time for number one!
Things go to my head
With breakfast in bed
And I indulge in treats
With no deadline to beat.
Because you see my dears,
For the first time in years
I am waiting on me;
Just my cup of tea.

Lucretia Lang

MY RETIREMENT MOVE

Micawber style my money flows
How long 'twill last inflation knows!
To sell, to buy, to rent? I cry,
In answer comes a heavy sigh;
My maths are pure precision
But conjure no decision.

The die is cast at last my friend,
To pastures new my footsteps wend.
I cannot stay to count the cost
In known ways and faces lost;
Since pounds and pence must rule my style
I take my leave with cheerful smile,
My fears and feelings of regret
Well hidden for I'm smiling yet.

Hermione Cole

LATE SPRING

Love in late life, the ultimate twinkle;
Fairies dancing on a dusty window-pane;
Quince and cream for breakfast
On a drab Lent morning;
September sunlight playing on a quiet carpet
Of brown and yellow leaves.
Hearts meet for the last time.
Hushed words of love fall like fading petals
Onto the dark ripples of a deep pool.
Pale lips silently mouth the jumbled memories
Of a thousand half-forgotten
Sentimental songs.
Shall we dance?
Shall we waltz away this twilight time
To the sound of slow music?
And later, shall we make love?. . .
Eyes tightly closed against the light,
Bodies straining urgently
To electrify the night.
Just for old-time's sake, let us
Paint rainbows in the cypress grove,
Run barefoot, with cold toes,
Through the distant water-meadow,
Seeking, once again, late spring sunshine,
To linger where the sky is always blue,
Where bright stars shine by day,
And nightingales listen as we whisper,
'Can this be really you?'

M Morales

HOW I YEARN

I wish, how I wish,
I was young yet again.
All slight and slim,
Yes, nimble of limb.
Fleet of the foot,
And as sure of it, too.
Fresh as the rosebud
That's glistening with dew.
Joyous of heart, and
Yes, gladsome of mind.
Seeking adventures,
They're so hard to find.
Wondering what lurks
Round every corner I turn.
Oh, for those carefree days
Of my youth, how I yearn!

I yearn, how I yearn
Just to live free of care.
To flash with a smile, and
With bright eyes beguile.
To swing with the pelvis.
Or sway with the hips.
To pout with the mouth
Thus to tempt with red lips.
Light of the spirit,
All free of the soul.
Ambling through life
Without any set goal.
Ignorant of heartache,
Of suffering, of pain.
Oh! For the magic of youth
I wish I was young yet again!

Dorothy Hitchman

FEELING YOUNG

I don't *feel* fat and sixty six
But slim and thirty three
As I go cycling down the lane
Greeting friends I see.

My knees may ache when it is cold
My hair is now quite grey,
But I forget the passing years
And savour every day.

The march of time goes on and on
Like waves upon the sea,
What matters is the way I feel
Right here inside of me.

Edna Cosby

A NEW LEASE OF LIFE

I reached the age of fifty plus
Now that has passed me by,
I must fulfil the rest of my life
Not sit around and cry.

There are many things I wish to do
But time just goes so quick,
I will try to tell you some of them
If it helps you just a bit.

I go to collect my pension
Then off to do a big spend,
But now I am over sixty
It is a problem to bend.

Apart from all the usual chores
And different meals to cook,
I can sit in front of the Telly!
Or read a jolly good book.

I like to play the organ
Or paint a picture or two,
A jigsaw or a game of chess
Write poems like this one for you.

Do a bit of gardening
Swim at the local pool,
Go out with friends on an outing
My freedom is my jewel!

It is great to be over sixty
With memories by the score,
I have my lovely grandchildren
I could not wish for more.

There are many more to mention
Now I am sixty plus,
Everyone will get a chance
As it comes to all of us!

Marlene Gilbert

SWEET SIXTY AND NEVER SWEETER!

S-Sixty the age of a retiring society, if you're a girl!
I-Invalid for some, but I'd still give things a whirl
X-Xcitement is still high on my list
T-Talent with wise thoughts and memories at the flick of a wrist
Y-You haven't seen anything yet, life has just begun for me,

S-Sixty one sixty two and I'll still be the same at eighty three!
O-Only worries left will be those of family affairs
M-Money's no option with my stocks and my shares
E-Entertainment is easy give me a film on TV
T-Time on my hands to help raise money for a charity
H-Handy hints to hand down the ages I find as I clear out
I-Intelligent computer and technology make me shout!
N-Not in my day I feel my age now
G-Gold help us! To enjoy all the time he'll allow.

Debra Neale

PONDERINGS OF AGE

If I could say something profound
No reason would I need to wonder
Why in my youth, my ideas did abound,
Yet age brought me reasons to ponder.

I wonder then on my past life
Whilst counting the goals I achieved
Then question the struggles and occasional strife
And what it was I so believed.

We bring nothing with us at birth
Nor can we take anything out.
But is what I've done, been of such worth
It proved what birth's cry was about?

Grace Leeder-Jackson

BAND OF GOLD

Since you placed this band of gold upon my finger, Further back in time than
I would care to say,
We've shared the years together, where have they gone? It seems
like only yesterday,
That we stood before the alter, and made our vow's as man and wife,
These vow's that we are mindful of, and will keep throughout our life,
We never needed others, it was sufficient that I had you,
The road was sometimes stony, but we helped each other through,
We always did something special, when our anniversary came round,
We wanted folks to know about the happiness we'd found,
There is much to celebrate, in the years that have gone by,
We've always been true to each other, you and I,
I don't understand today's morals, and wonder if they cared,
About the simple pleasures we have, and the love that we have shared,
It's not been all sunshine, Oh no, don't get me wrong,
Our troubles have been like ripples on a stream, put in proportion, where
they belong,
The magic words for me were, to have and to hold,
Ever since that day, I've worn your precious band of gold.

Val Matthews

AGED SIXTY FIVE

Happy birthday mother dear
You are sixty five today
Ooh mum you have a wrinkle or two
No son they are called laughter lines
Ooh mum you are going grey
No son it's called going silver
Mu-um you have put on weight
Yes son it's just another worry for my age
Dearest mother will I be like you
When I am sixty five
Laughter lines silver hair plump
No son you will have different worries
Because my son I am a Mum.

Lily Robinson

ME AT SIXTY TWO

When I was young and in my prime,
and sixty was 'just old',
Someone to look up to
While doing what I'm told.

But now the hands of time have turned
and I am now 'Just old',
Whatever happened to the years
Between the grey and gold?

I find people treat me kindly
as they respect my age
I stumble almost blindly
into an even greater age.

I've learned so much from books and such
I'm still learning every day
Though I do it much more slowly
So I turn another page.

I've had pain and laughter, tears and so much joy
days full of sunshine, and others full of rain
have I really learned so much
or would I do it all again?

G Edwards

FREEDOM

It's grand to be sixty - and a little bit more,
The office seems so far away,
No more computers and modems and printers,
(and gossip behind a closed door)

Now I can have my breakfast at nine,
Read all the news at my leisure,
Have two cups of tea and take one up with me.
To bathe and to dress with such pleasure.

I can garden and mow,
Take cuttings that grow,
Write letters or simply go out,
I can study the market,
Take the car out and park it,
Without having to go round and round.

It may be a myth,
But I sometimes feel stiff,
And sometimes I feel rather tired,
But what do I care,
I can sit in my chair,
And have forty winks in the quiet.

Cynthia Fenwick

REFLECTIONS BY THE POND

They pass me by, they know me not
And I know none of them
As I sit here in pensive mood
Recalling old times when
Familiar faces passed this way
And greetings we exchanged
Discussed our children's progress
And meetings we arranged.
Nostalgic thoughts pass through my mind
Of happy days long gone,
Warm summer days with birdsong
Cold winter's ice and snow
The swish of skates on frozen pond
Young faces all aglow.
Now ducks and ducklings cross the pond
With raucus quacking noise
Knowing they'll be fed again
By friendly girls and boys.
I walk away from willow trees
Which gently sway in summer breeze
Take one last look at mothers there
With smiling children on their knees.
One day they'll be as old as I
The best years oh' so swiftly fly
With silent thoughts I wish them well,
Good health, good luck, good-bye.

Q Fowles

THE BIG 60

OK so it's my birthday
I've reached the big 60
now you must treat me gently
help me when I'm slow.

Now I've got a good excuse
when I don't quite know
what it means or what to do
show me where to go

OK so don't pity me
don't think me a bore
when you're so enjoying life
I've done it all before.

Joan Berriman

SIXTY SOMETHING

Now that I am nearly sixty
It's not quite so much fun,
As when I was much younger
And only twenty one.

There was so much to look forward to
Or so at least I thought,
Instead I got married and had children,
Now they have children of their own.

The moral of this story is,
If there is anything you really want to do.
The world is there for you to explore,
Go on and do it before your twenty four.

E C Williams

CLICKITY CLICK - SIX FAT LADIES

Sixty years young.
Father and Son.
Man and Boy,
been returning here,
along the Pier.

Hold her, point her say 'Look out to sea'.
This is where I stood
same spot.
Can't say it hasn't changed a jot.

Now I'm Sixty
and you are sixteen
months.
Grinning at your
Granfer.
I'm putting thoughts into
your tiny curly head,
relinquished from mine.
Such is the difference
between us.
Now reason
has ripened with all the many
passing seasons.

Cora Tanner

REFLECTIONS OF A LIFE

To penetrate through misty eyes, and breach the vale of time.
To pace the path of all my dreams, and reach a time sublime,
I see my childhood flash my eyes, cascades of joyous play,
Safely in my carefree world, undaunted day by day . . .
Excited in my childish way, my spirit soaring high,
I plundered through that youthful maze, adulthood to defy.
War came, the bubble burst, the battle thunders through,
And all my happy, carefree days, became so precious few.
Then with the peace, I settled down, to ponder lifetimes role,
To elevate my place in life, though never reaching goal,
I look back over this, my life, as I reach my shadow years.
A path defines my autumn scene, where rest and peace appears.
Yet if I strode that path again, that pulsing, coursing vein.
I'll see again the friends I knew, life's dream would start again.

Thomas Victor Healey

THE OLD BANGER

The old banger has done lots of miles;
Now, it causes more tears than smiles.
When it's cold, it just won't start;
The old thing's nearly falling apart.
The boot won't close; the doors are stiff;
Maybe I'll push it over the cliff.

When I awake it's hard to start,
To bend my knees and pump my heart.
There's a pain all down my back,
And my hair is no longer black.
My diet keeps me rumbling with hunger.
Oh well, I'll never be any younger.

I decided to fix the old car,
So I could travel near and far,
The doors close easily with a bit of oil;
The boot will close after a lot of toil.
The motor now is working fine,
The paint was changed to the colour of wine.

Maybe I should do the same for myself
By taking better care of my health,
I'll start to work on my weaker points,
Like exercise to loosen my joints;
With any luck, I'll still be alive,
Long after I've passed sixty-five!

Rosemary Taylor

A CELEBRATION

When I reached the age of sixty,
I thought 'Well this is it,
I will go upstairs and lie down,
In a dark room for a bit.'
I thought about my bus pass,
And then my old age pension,
But a loud knocking at my door,
Proved a timely intervention.

Outside were all the family,
In glorious array,
'Get your glad rags on mum,
This is your special day,
You are not on your last legs yet,
Whatever you may think,
You do not need a walking stick,
To come out for a drink'.

A session in the nearest pub,
With tales of days gone by,
And soon we all had handkerchiefs,
There wasn't a dry eye,
They say life begins at forty,
But it does at sixty too,
And if anyone thinks differently,
They haven't got a clue.

I could join the over sixties club,
They have outings by the score,
This is my chance to live it up,
And go out and explore,
No longer feelings of self pity,
With tongue in cheek I've wrote this ditty.

Jean Goodman

BEING SIXTY

You're not really old
When you retire
You have more time
And plenty more fire
You don't have to worry
About going to work
What to wear
Or what shirt.

You can go out
And do as you please
Whether to have coffee
Or cups of teas
No children you have
Under your feet
They'll be plenty new friends
That you can meet.

You can have fun
Now that you're free
And just remember
Your only Sixty

Mary-Ann Adams

SIXTY PLUS

Hip, hip, hip, hip, hooray!
I'm sixty plus this day.
I've left the rat race,
To go at my own pace.
I'm free! Free! Free!
You'll get fed up, the pessimists warned.
Who me? When a new life has dawned.
On your bike, mister. I'll enjoy this life.
No more worries, no more strife.
I'm free! Free! Free!
Seventy plus and looking back.
What took me off my track?
Family, always phoning, always there.
They mean well. It's just because they care.
They seem to think I'm lonely,
Not feeding myself so well.
They love me dearly, but if only
They'd let me be to dwell,
On the things I long to do.
My neighbours say I'm lucky
To have my family there.
Making sure I'm quite alright,
Showing that they care.
I love you dearly, family,
All I ask is space, space to be
A soul set free. Don't smother me!

R E E Thurley

THE LESSON OF LIFE

When you are sixteen life's full of strife
Uncertainty looms, what to do with your life?
At twenty it's better, you're learning the ropes.
Well on the road with a heart full of hopes.
Married by thirty or carving career,
Regretting mistakes but still filled with cheer.
At age forty nine you are settling down
But the big 5-0's coming causing a frown.
Take heart all you youngsters the best is to come
For life after fifty can be lots of fun.
You've found your own style and you're looking divine.
You've matured at last like the finest of wine.
The whole of your life is a challenge to face,
So don't rush the fences, just make your own pace.
Savour the moment of each passing decade
Build mountains of memories, don't let them fade.
And when you look back on what you have done.
Of battles you've fought and victories won.
Don't waste time on regrets, bless the lessons you've learned,
Now you can relax and enjoy all you've earned.

B Marcucci

RETIREMENT

'I dread the day you retire,' my good wife said to me,
'You must think hard, and take up an interesting hobby.
I don't want you under my feet all day, you'll get in the way,
Especially when I hoover, and dust, hang out the clothes on washing day.'

'Well my dear, I can peel the spuds, and prepare the veg,
I'll try not to get in the way, and put your nerves on edge,
In the summer I can rake and hoe, clean all the paths,
Potter about in the greenhouse, and sweep down the yard.'

'It's the Winter time I dread the most,' she says with a gleam in her eye,
'When it's cold and wet, the East wind blows, and the snow begins to lie,'
'Well dear, we can go for walks together, along the shore and pines,
When it's frosty, and cold, and the winter sun does shine.'

I'd secretly longed to retire for many a year,
Put up my feet, and enjoy life without a care,
Get up when I like, and do just as I please,
In fact, do my level best, to live a life of ease.

It's now 20 months since that happy day arrived,
Time has flown by, 'Where has it gone,' I gently sighed,
I've confounded the wife, I've found plenty to do,
Traced my family tree, read Norfolk's history, my interests grew.

As you can see, I've also decided to write the odd rhyme,
It's all good fun, and it helps pass the time,
Keeps the brain ticking over, stops me from falling asleep,
Even if this pathetic doggerel, makes my poor wife weep.

David Bunting

SIXTY SOMETHING

Sixty something is not a good age to be
When you have had a busy life
Now there's just 'Afternoon tea',
I miss the kids running around us
wanting this and that,
'Mum, can you get me some dinner?'
'Dad, can you mend my bat?'
Those hectic days are now over
Now we are quite alone
So at least we can keep the garden in trim
And buy something nice for the home
Our lifestyle is quite different now,
Nothing is quite the same,
We'll keep taking those vitamins
I'm not having that 'Zimmer Frame'
We've got the company of each other now,
Something we haven't had for years
Even if people do look at us
And say 'Look at that pair of old dears'.

Pam Newman

SIXTY SOMETHING +

What's that you say? I can't hear you see.
All right - you don't have to shout at me.
Oh dear! My poor legs, they feel so weak, -
I wish you would be quiet and let *me* speak.
My stomach's all upset, I've got such a pain,
Now it's my head that is aching again.
My back hasn't been right since I fell over the mat,
I have to be careful not to trip over the cat,
My poor hands are so sore, I can't touch a thing,
It's even a job to keep wearing my ring.
My chest is so tight - you can hear it rattle,
To even take a breath is quite a battle.
My arms are so heavy I can't lift them high
No matter how often and hard I do try.
My shoulders are bowed more and more each day
And the hairs on my head are all turning grey.
Why! Oh Why! Do I feel so cold?
Do you suppose it's because I am old?

June Rogers

OLD AGE

Old age must come
To everyone
There's no escape
For anyone
So when you stop
And wonder why
That your life
Has passed you by
And if it makes you
Feel so sad
Remember your life
And the good times
You have had.

Alan Green

WHAT IS AGE

What is age? It is a number in our mind,
Some are old, at sixty this I find.
But then there is the young at heart,
At sixty for them, life will start.

A cheerful word, a gentle smile,
These are our gifts, that make life worthwhile.
As you go along life's road,
Think about your highway code.

To your neighbour, smile as you pass by,
Not a groan or burden with a sigh.
Then you without, a doubt will see,
How catching a smile can be.

A cheerful smile, a happy face,
Can make all the difference, in the human race.
No matter how old or young we are,
We all like catching, a falling star.

So start each day; think young at heart,
Because this is where, our day does start.
Then think how different, life to all would be
If a smile on our neighbour's face we see.

V M Foulger

SIXTY SOMETHING

If only I were younger,
It would give me so much cheer,
For where I used to be in front,
I'm now back at the rear.
Things all take so much longer,
My bones need oil in plenty,
They creek and crack,
and Oh! My back,
It wasn't like this at twenty,
Oh well! I grin and bear it,
With friends who feel the same.
Our brains still keep on working,
I think it's such a shame.

Phyllis Mason

THE GREY HAIRED OLD MAN

There is a grey haired old man looking lost and alone
Sitting crouched at the door of his home
Looking for a smile or a nod to come his way
Just a friendly greeting to brighten his day.

It is so sad to see him sit there.
Is there nobody in this world to care,
Nobody with his life he can share
No friends or family with time to spare.

When the sun goes down at the end of the day.
In he will go and alone he will stay.
If you happen to see him there
Give him a smile and a kind word pay.

I Barton

THE GRIM REAPER

Look up into the sky
At the army racing past,
Can you hear the screams?
The future's fleeing so fast.

Look up into the blue,
Feel the breeze on your face,
Can you live with yourself
As you falter in the race?

A hovering Kestrel screams
Dancing death in the sky,
Don't you wish you could hover
And soar where the eagles fly?

Look at the ground you hover above,
Look at all that nature beneath,
Full hungry for birth as nature unearths
And then lies to rest her wreath.

Soon a darkness claim your soul,
The curtain of the final act,
There will be no more exits, no more entrances,
Sans everything and that's a fact.

But you've led a rich life and,
You've done exactly what we expect,
Now it's time to retire the crown
Because the Reaper wants you next.

Matthew James Friday

GROWING OLD

If we could start again without our birth a matter of contention
The changes it would make to us are too numerous to mention
For we have a built-in computer that is fed with information
And with almost all we do age seems to influence the equation
Some information fed to us we should never have been told
And we must try our utmost for it to release the hold
Education starts at a certain age and we leave when it's complete
And now we must go into the world and be ready to compete
Some are ready some are not to face the unexpected
You may be told you're old enough though what you've learned is
                                                      not connected
And so you begin to see that age will always be a factor
Whether you become an engineer or politician or even possibly an actor
Someone suggested a span of life and no doubt it was well meant
But we will never know how this affects each one on how their life is spent
The experiences we go through can be made use of at different stages
For some accomplish many things more relevant to their ages
We hear remarks also that a person could be old before their time
Which could mean that for part of that life was no reason or little rhyme
But if we didn't know our age we would always have a go
Yet the advice 'be very careful' is one that most of us will know
That our age has been recorded is a fact we must concede
But the pleasure in achieving is one we will always need
So we can still continue to ignore the three score years and ten
And when the time comes to give up then we will tell them when

Reginald Morris

RELEASED FROM TIME

In hours of childhood I read books,
While a kettle gently hissed on a glowing stove
This time has returned,
While others hurry to work
I sip my coffee and gently muse.
Time is mine, no more enquiring looks
When work is not completed to line.

Each day a holiday
I float amidst the busy throng,
enthralled with every aspect of life
Watching children's games,
the breathless beauty of flowers,
and hearing music's sound.

At home the printed word is at my bidding.
And hours of cosiness and pleasure spent.
Movement is my choice, and where to walk.
Every day is a holiday.

Joan Skinner

CHATTER

There's nothing I like better
Than a good old get together
With friends I haven't see for many years.
We gossip and we natter, we criticise and flatter
And we talk about our many hopes and fears.
We talk about the good old days
Before we went our separate ways
When we were young and foolish, sometimes bad
And it doesn't seem to matter,
All the wrinkles and the flabber
'Cos we're girls again, what smashing times we had.
The years between just melt away
And we are young and very gay.
We never gave thought of the tomorrow
Or even of the things that could bring sorrow.
But have another drink my friends before we part again
And raise our glasses up to days we wish to free from pain
For we are getting older now, but girls we'll always be
If we still think and try to see the world as it once used to be.

Wyn Sear

SIXTY SOMETHING

I heard a friend of mine remark
That she was sixty three
And then I thought Oh my God
That will soon be me.

Now when I was a little girl
That was as old as old can be
But now it doesn't matter
Because I know I'm me

So isn't it a miracle
That while the outside decays
The blithe and youthful spirit
Within us still remains

So if you think that's funny
Just listen and be told
If you always feel young inside
You never will grow old

Old is just a body
Young is what you are
To hell with my old body
I'm younger still by far

Edna D'Lima

OLD FRIENDS

Life is just a fleeting glance
that passes all too quick,
we either know great happiness
or just a little chink.

Growing old has been no fun
our laughter turned to tears,
we moan as we watch the sun
set on our passing years.

But friendship is a thing we know
for just a little while,
may we meet again someday
when we have learned to smile.

Annie Ramsay Pryde

OLD ON THE STREET

Warm blankets dry me
Warm arms touch me
Warm soup tells me
That I'm still alive.

Warm hands tend me
Warm faces smile at me,
So why do I feel
So cold inside?

Andrew Francis Collett

AT LAST

This is my news at sixty plus,
nothing has changed, well not that much.
Food is still inviting, men still enticing,
music high on the list.
Acrobatics I desist
The world around is still in a mess,
but I haven't time for all that stress.
Everyday there's some-thing new, I'm busy
doing, what I like to do.
Nothing special, nothing intense, pleasing
          myself, content.
It's my time now to live as I choose,
and that my friend is the
end of the news.

I D Welch

WHO IS THAT STRANGER?

I look in the mirror, a stranger looks my way,
How could I change that much from yesterday?
I don't like what I see when life has just begun,
The frame's folding' up on me, but the heart is ever young!

The eyes are puffy, the cheeks sunken in,
Loose flesh on the neck, gopher pockets ride the chin,
The eyes close resting on my face,
Eyes that see my all and have known God's grace.

I dare to look again at eyes that look at me,
The softness that I see jars my memory,
I pat the deep lines, Q-tips them with putty,
But I can't fool the stranger mimicking me!

I start laughing at the stranger in the mirror,
The stranger laughs with me until we both shed tears,
But only my laughter reaches my ears,
The stranger laughs silently and sheds dry tears.

I kiss the stranger, the kiss comes back to me.
We wink at each other simultaneously,
I whisper, 'You old son-of-a-gun,
The frame's folding' up on me, but the heart is ever young.'

Janice Burns

78

SIXTY SOMETHING

When I was sixty something, I started to ski
I soon was to learn, speed and sliding were not for me
My boots weighed a ton, and the ski's over your shoulder, should be
I struggled to the slopes, not far
When a voice said, here you are
you are supposed to carry your own ski's you know
but we made it at last on the lovely white snow
then I called to my son . . . I must have photo
He got out his camera . . . but I said, Oh don't leave go!
I wanted to prove, that I'd had a go . . . with pictures to show

We went up the mountain in a lift chair
with feet dangling in mid air
it didn't stop
when we reached the top
We had to jump off with great care
but it was well worthwhile when we got there
It was a glorious view with the bright warm sun, shining
on happy skiers everywhere

Stand on the back of my ski's, said my son
just to get the hang of moving, Mum
He teaches skiing and thinks it's great fun
He knew really . . . I would never, ever, do the Red Run!
It was great, for a few yards, til we picked up speed
then I broke the ski rule and tensed up . . . I did indeed
Oh dear, Oh dear, over we did go . . .
suddenly . . . a great heap we were, in the snow
I laughed and I cried at the same time, but now I know
It is said that it is never too late . . . but I still don't want to go

Edna Parrington

WOMEN RETIRE AT 60 . . .

I wonder how many married women like me
Thought that on reaching the 'ripe old age' of 60,
The pension would be for them to collect
No hitch nor a problem did they detect.

But . . .

Men qualify at age sixty five years
Women at sixty - I had no fears
Since marriage I have been housewife and mum,
Cook, gardener, nurse, cleaner, to name only some
of the unpaid jobs on twenty-four hour call:
But in spite of this, I've no pension at all!

Yet . . .

I have to wait 'till I'm sixty-four
When my husband collects his at one year more
It is only women who have worked for wages
And paid for a stamp at weekly stages
Who get the pension. However, it's not unfair
My husband has paid for me to be there -

Eventually . . .

My quarrel is with the misleading saying,
Without qualification, that women need to be paying
The wording should be for clarification
'Some women retire at 60' then there's no prevarication

Hopefully!

Margaret C Cobb

80

REACHING SIXTY

At the moment I am fifty five
But I feel so very much alive
And when I reach my sixtieth year
I'll do it without an ounce of fear

I'll do the things I haven't done
I know it will be lots of fun
I'm looking forward to leisure time
To have a lie-in will be fine

I'll sign on at a night-school class
I'll study hard and exams I'll pass
I've always wanted to learn a language
So I'll listen to tapes whilst having a sandwich

To write a book would be just fine
I'll do it as I'll have the time
I'll visit places I've not seen before
Who could ask for anything more?

To have an early morning run
To me that would be lots fun
I'll exercise and get in shape
No need to hurry and say 'I'm late'

At one time sixty I thought I'd dread
But now I know I can look ahead
And plan the things I've dreamed I'd do
For being sixty will make it come true.

Janet McBride

AN OLD YOUNG STUD...

A happy light a shooting star,
A bright summer haze, wherever you are.
I loved you right away when we first met.
When you said you'd stay I just couldn't forget.
We found love so tender, yet satisfying and wild.
Yet I'm sixty five, you're twenty, just a child.
You said I'm your young stud, that's how you make me feel
Though how long will you be happy with me, is my last chance real?
I hope when my life is at its end,
You're there to say goodbye, and will still love me my friend,
Though even if you've gone like a will o' the whisp,
Your memory will live on, bright sunny and crisp.
Weather you stay or not I'm happy we two,
Found whatever we have, and I'll always love you . . .

Gwen McNamara

LIFE

People rushing to and fro
Others with nowhere to go
Laughing crying hurrying on
Looking for what lies beyond
Ever seeking that endless quest
Sweet contentment
Life they say is often sweet
Sharing joy with those we meet
Giving strength where there is need
Always conscious of the greed
That makes us selfish too
But when we give we will receive
A friendship strong and true

Christine Ferguson

ONE DAY WHILST I WASN'T LOOKING

One day whilst I wasn't looking
My hair became thinner,
Tummy fatter, children taller, me smaller.
The world seemed to be in fifth gear
Instead of just ticking over.
Black and white became multicoloured,
More words changed their meaning:
Like - gay and pot, shoot and squat
Marriage is no-longer encouraged,
To get into debt is!
One day whilst I wasn't looking
I got older.

Neville Hawkins

REFLECTIONS IN LIFE'S MIRROR

Who can this dear old lady be
sitting dreaming in her chair?
Can it be me - but young no more -
with this wealth of silvery hair?

In my heart I know I feel
forever young - *have* I grown old?
Where's the girl who used to be
laughing, carefree - very bold?
Who took on life, and all its knocks,
who set too, faced up to things,
dealt with problems - where is she?
The time sped by on unseen wings,
so swift, so silent. I paid no heed.
Now only the memories remain
gilded over, or with a veneer -
the bad times forgotten, and the pain.

Only pleasurable things are here to recall,
bright episodes down the road of life,
so precious, so dear, loving thoughts of
when I was a daughter, mother, wife.

J Hockley

AND A GOLD WATCH TOO

I wake up in the morning
and my bones they start to creak
I have to think what date it is
And what day of the week.

I draw the curtains, see the rain
then toddle off downstairs
My wife says 'Milk's gone sour again
and I've got no bread for toast'.

The dog is waiting by the door
His eyes are all aglow
Insisting on his daily walk
Whether or not I want to go.

Bedraggled, wet, with aching feet
Trudging past a pub still shut,
Hungry and cold, go down the street
Behind that crazy mutt.

Arrive back home, forgotten my key
My wife's having forty winks.
So it's into the garage for me and the dog,
And there I sits and thinks.

Oh joy of being sixty-five
But rebellious thoughts do lurk.
Can I be happy just once more,
Please, can I go back to work.

Peter Gormally

I'M STILL YOUR SWEETHEART

Is it just a few years, since you called sweetheart,
And told me you loved me, and gave me your heart.
Is it just a few years, since your face filled with joy,
As you held in your arms, our sweet baby boy.

Is it just a few years, since you made love to me,
And told, you would love me, through eternity.
Is it just a few years, since you gave me a hug,
Now you push me away with a frown or a shrug.

Is it just a few years, since we stopped our small talk,
Now we just watch TV, never go for a walk.
Is it just a few years, since you stopped loving me,
Though I am older and greyer, my love, I'm still me.

Dorothy Laming

SIXTY SOMETHING

I am sixty three
and approaching retirement age
I am like any old book
with torn pages.
I am five foot eight
and fit as a fiddle
Retirement age
I think is just in the middle
I like music
and like to dance
Ho! Though I am sixty three
I still enjoy work and a good romance
I like my beer
and like to dine
I always enjoy my food
With a glass of wine
over the years
I tried to do what I could
But in life, we always
To the old proverbs return
Which say, the older you get
The more you will learn.
One day the retirement age
will finally come
I hope I can still enjoy myself
And have some fun.
I appreciate material things in life
I do confess
But I think most important
Is a very good health.

Saverio Pozella

RETIRED

Retirement age has come at last
It's time to take a rest
You haven't got to rush about
But do the things, you love the best

Like working in the garden
Cutting grass and pottering in the shed
You've planted out the garden
And the paper you have read

You tidy up your fencing
And creosote as well
The gutter needed cleaning
Cause off the steps I fell

We now have time to go away
We couldn't do before
Like go away on holiday
And lock the blinking door

Now after getting home again
We tidy around once more
Like cut the grass and weeding
Then get ready for a tour.

Bert Salter

AGE CONCERN

From nifty fifty approaching sixty
Life can still keep you in sane.
You get your act together, map out your week ahead.

Monday swimming that's what I said.
Tuesday is tea dancing, I should have a ball
In Widnes at the Royal Queen's hall.

Wednesday is pay-day to the post office and queue
Weekly pension - thank you.
Friday is tap dancing, drama too
No matter what age, there's something for you.

Saturday, shopping sometimes a bore.
But happy if grandchild comes knocking upon door.
A stroll in the park, walking the dog.
Visit the library, town hall or pub.

Sixty doesn't make you feel old.
It's the prime of your life, so I've been told.
With so much to do, and so much to see.
Time on your hands to make you feel free.
The choice is yours feel young or old.
What ever you see, will be.

Gail Rowan

ON REFLECTION

He looked straight in my eyes spoke not a word,
Yet told me the facts of the case
Your brows showing wrinkles, your mouth is drawn in
Your cheekbones, protruding, more so when you grin.
Your eyes showing bloodshot; the blue turning grey
And now, you've more forehead, where once there was hair

Looking straight back at him, I knew it was true,
Concerning his views on my face
My eyes now are sunken, dark shadows beneath,
Thin lips proclaiming the loss of my teeth
Furrows, and wrinkles, and dark hollow places,
Could not be hid at this meeting of faces

I could not deny it, the hair all but grey,
Deep ugly ditches, 'Once laughter lines lay
Oh! How the truth of this awful collection
Had come to light, in this mirror reflection.

Frank Hewer

MY RETIREMENT

You're working days are over so said the boss
And I know the company will suffer your loss.
How lovely those words sounded to me
I'm 60 years old and at last I'm free
To do all the things I want to do
And not be told it's no good for you
I'll travel and see all the great works of art
Not having to hurry back will be the best part
I'll visit the opera where all the greats sing
Perhaps I too could have a fling
I'll eat at the best restaurants and try the posh food
If I don't like it though, I'd better not be rude.
I'll take up swimming for exercise you see
On second thoughts that costume looks awful on me
I'll wear the latest fashions, they're sure to look good
And have my hair styled by Sassoon as every woman should.
I'll visit the grandkids and give them all my love
As only a loving grandma could
But before all this, there's one thing I must do
I'll go to church and say a big thank you
For giving me the chance to make my dreams come true
Before it's time to rest in Heaven surrounded by
Love from you

Kathryn Bassindale

AUNT EVE

At seventeen she joined the ATS
I bet she had all the girls laughing in their mess
On leave her sister Pam's clothes she would borrow
If they were brand new she told Pam Oh you can wear them tomorrow.

Eve met and married George after the war they were married a good
few years
For him two lovely children she did bare
Eve is now sixty plus
On her own don't make a fuss,
She lives life to the full and holidays she does enjoy
Eve would keep up with any toy-boy,
Loves dancing all the mod steps she a great mover,
Then that's when all the men's eyes do a rover,
Her monthly meals out with the girls,
In a new dress she gives them a twirl
She so young at heart she thinks she twenty-one,
I hope she keeps up her life so full of fun.

D J Newman

THE AUTUMN YEARS

The Autumn years
The final years
Brought many tears
But decision made
I'm not afraid
To stay alone
All on my own
Start life anew
Without you
Now I'm sixty-two.

Franie Yoller

WHAT SORT OF THINGS DO OLD PEOPLE DO?

What sort of things do old people do?
They were all young once like me and you,
They might think back to their younger days,
And relive their merry months of Mays.

Do they prefer to be old or young?
Does it hurt to think about their mum?
Would they rather leave the past alone?
Remember memories on their own.

What other things do old people do?
Did they want to know like me and you?
Or just find out when their old day came?
And just sit and bear rheumatic pains.

What things do the old enjoy to do?
Buying sweets for their grandchildren too,
Going on holiday, giving treats,
And walking their dogs around the streets.

Spending money they took years to earn,
They left school years too early to learn,
They still remember old money and,
These new coins are like a foreign land!

Dawn Lennon

GETTING OLDER

Fast approaching sixty
I feel it every day
The wrinkles on my face
Are definitely here to stay
But that is just the down side
The best is yet to come
Soon I'll be retiring
And I'm going to have some fun.

Sylvia White

HURRAY! IT'S ON ITS WAY

Retirement now is not far away
I will be home each and every day
Time to spend in the garden keeping it neat
Or sit in the armchair just resting my feet

It will not matter what time I rise in the morning
If I do not go to bed until a new day is dawning
My days will no longer follow a set routine
There will be time to go places yet unseen

To clear out the sheds and make them tidy
Can be done any day then Monday to Friday
There will be time for a game of golf to play
And on the course all day I can stay

Jobs around the house that have to be done
Will not be a chore I shall find them fun
Spend more time with my nose in a good book
Who knows I may even learn to cook!

So I am looking forward to this time with pleasure
Doing all I want at my own pace and with leisure
I can look back on nearly fifty years of working
No wonder dreams of retirement in my mind are lurking

Mavis Stoker

OLD AGE

Make time your friend
Walk with him,
At his pace.
Take each step;
At his measure.

Then arm in arm,
Life's journey through,
Each day you'll truly treasure.

For he's not here to harm you,
And he's been here before.
Don't try to overtake him,
By rushing through life's door.

There is no rest for him you see;
He travels night and day.
He smiles at youth;
Frowns at old age,
And never stops to stay.

Make time your friend;
Where ere you be
Walk gently on together.
And when a man,
With sandals calls
He'll let you go forever.

Windsor Hopkins

A SELF-EMPLOYED PENSIONER

It was only just a month ago
I finally reached the big 'Six-oh'.
I had every intention
Of enjoying my pension
And letting the world by me flow!

There were lots of plusses I thought I could see
In becoming a 'working' OAP.
I'd accept every perk
I would work, or I'd shirk
When I liked - now who could prevent me?

But so far it hasn't worked out quite like that.
I hardly ever have time for a chat.
I'm still typing all day
In the old hectic way.
Nothing's changed - and that is a fact!

Lucy M Kaye

INDELIBLE MEMORIES

Indelible memories, that can never be erased
Might seem like only yesterday
Or back in far-off days
Perhaps a faded photograph
Or a tune you chance hear
Will maybe bring a smile
Or possibly a tear

A holiday, forgotten 'till a friend you chance to meet
Then you reminisce about the fun
Whilst chatting in the street
The children, then, were very young
They're all married now
But how the memories linger on
What stories they can tell

But the memory most indelible
Is of the courting days
When life was fun, and we were young
And the sun was out - always.

Where have all the years gone?
They have slipped by Oh! So fast
But memories stay, in some strange way
Reminders of the past
I know my book of memories
Will never ever fade,
Because the ink's indelible
With happiness it's made.

V Tank

SIXTY-TWO

Were not sure of what to do
We have a future but not in full view.
Finding new interests that's what we'll do
Our minds have a plan thinking it through, having more time.
Having more rest, at sixty-two it's one of the best.

Margaret Brown

WHAT'S IT ALL ABOUT - BEING SIXTY

It's ordering books from the library and when the payment's due
Being asked 'Are you on concession', can they possibly mean you!
It's days I feel it's all downhill, and don't I look a mess
When for the umpteenth time that week I can't fasten my dress
It's when my makeup fails to hide the wrinkles of the years
And the thought of mutton dressed as lamb, becomes a constant fear
It's being chatted up by men old enough to be my dad
Then remembering we met at school, when they were just a lad
It's wondering what happened to the girl so fancy free
I know she dwells inside me, still feeling twenty three
It's having 'Himself' at home all day, no chance to be alone
I must admit it's nice though, I really shouldn't moan
It's taking life less seriously, sitting in the sun
And if something interesting comes up, the housework isn't done
It's seeing more of my family and their house renovation
I'm an expert now at building and their garden's a sensation
It's having time to call my own, free from work at last
And trying hard to make some sense in the memories of the past
It's wondering why I turned right instead of going left
Would life have been much different woven warp instead of weft
It's worrying will the money last and will I keep my health
For with the wisdom of the years, I know that it beats wealth
It's having youngsters ask me 'What happened in the war'
It seems another lifetime, for I was only four
It's accepting life's not a rehearsal as far as I can tell,
So I do my thing in my way the rest can go to Hell!

Gwendolyn Cameron

A BIT AFTER SIXTY

Sixty and a bit, what can I say,
I still 'think' thirty,
so why do I carry this tiring load about all day?
I speak slowly and clearly,
am quite calm in every way,
so why do I get patted and re-assured,
every step of the way?
My political opinions are up to date,
my daily affairs, I keep in a good state,
I drive a car, perhaps better than some,
so why on my birthday, are there so many
                        significant toasts?
I travel abroad,
take an interest in the community,
'Pop Music'? W-ell it's not really me.

Daphne Smith

PUSHING SIXTY

Soon I'll be sixty, and I can't wait,
I look at the calendar and tick off the date.
I'm planning already my leisure time
that wall clock's going, I never liked the chime.

It's a greenhouse for me and wellington boots,
cucumbers, lettuce, exotic fruits.
Winter holidays spent on the Costa Del Sol
to escape from the cold, a lovely long Hol'

Discount hairdos and a bus pass,
I'll be away that much I'll save on the gas.
Aerobics on Mondays to keep me fit,
there'll be no time to sit in my red and white kit.

Will I miss work when I retire?
No! I'll put up a sign saying 'This job for hire'.
You're as young as you feel on HRT,
life on the pension sounds alright to me!

Ruth Porritt

SIXTY PLUS

Birds are singing, the sun is bright,
We're having a party, here tonight.
There's plenty of food, champagne on ice,
We'll drink a toast, not once but thrice.
Why all the fuss, did I hear you say?
It's the beg seven '0', for me today.

What's it all about? I'll tell you for sure!
When I reached six '0', I wouldn't work no more,
Instead I'd watch TV and read some books.
But there's always something one overlooks,
A lifetime of action, suddenly turned to leisure,
Can bring more misery than it does pleasure.

One may be old but there's a door,
That will open wide, let you live once more.
Leads to many ways of finding pleasure,
And interests that, are beyond all measure.
Give a helping hand, where it is needed,
Experience and advice, is often heeded.

I may be slower, but I was not finished,
My faculties have as yet not diminished!
Into the wide world, I went once more,
Soon my spirits began to soar.
Now a decade on and still going strong,
Drop what you are doing and come along!

Les Reeves

SIXTY PLUS - SOS

What have I got to look forward to?
As sixty draws near, I think,
Where will I go, what will I do?
Will I dye my grey hair pink!

Will a coach come and take me off,
On a trip to the sea and sand?
Will I sit in a cafe and quickly scoff,
A cream cake, (clutching the change in my hand)!

Will I go to a hall, to hear people sing,
Try my hand at a game of Bingo?
I'm not really into that sort of thing,
But if I must, I'll have to learn the lingo!

Will I knit little squares for charity,
In a knitting afternoon?
If this is what sixty will mean to me,
Then seventy can't come too soon!

Meals on wheels, or the WI
I'd like to remain useful you see.
For even at sixty, I can't see why,
An old lady I'd have to be.

On the outside, I know we all start to look old,
With grey hair, and a wrinkle or two!
But inside we feel young, daring and bold,
And I'll not give in easy, Will you?

Denise Sanders

INDIAN SUMMER

When I was young, I used to be
careless about mortality.
I never thought of growing old,
With the aches and and pains that I'd been told
Would accompany the passing years,
Along with all the usual fears
Of being incapacitated
As body and mind deteriorated.
Now, here I am, at sixty plus,
Yet don't feel I have 'missed the bus'.
All right, so I have got arthritis
And even, occasional colitis,
But my mind's alert and going strong,
Holding its own among the throng.
I'm just as young in imagination
As I ever was, and in innovation
Feel I can hold the candle to youth,
Albeit, rather long in the tooth!
Age has its compensations, I've found,
It makes one less inhibition bound.
I question with impunity,
And take every opportunity
To challenge what I regard as can't.
I don't have to be a sycophant
To hold a job or please the public,
Now that I'm a geriatric.
I intend to carry on,
And if I can, live so long
That unless there's anything untowards,
I'll make the Guinness Book of Records!

B Gordon

NOT QUITE OVER THE HILL

I am in my late sixties, what more can I say
It is not very funny to be feeling this way
I have no longer a job to take up my time
I am an active man with no axe to grind.

My state pension just about covers our bills
I can fight off colds and the usual ills
My whole day is made up of various wishes
End up watching TV or cleaning the dishes.

My dear wife looks on rather bemused
Not quite sure of my movements or every day views
She does her best, on that I admit
Tries to maintain I am fighting fit.

The weather has a big part in my daily routine
If the rain persists fishing's out of the scene
The two dogs are restless, it's time for their walk
I meet others while walking and often we talk.

At the end of the day with the night creeping in
The cold left outside and the warmth kept within
There is really no complaints in respect of my day
It could have been harder, that's just the way.

Francis E Cockram

GROWING OLD WITH GRACE

In the rocking chair your eyes are closing,
It seems to me you're always dozing,
I look at you and what do I see,
A man who has aged quicker than me.

I won't give in to growing old,
Dye my hair, wear colours so bold,
Trying to keep my figure trim,
Telling myself I need to slim.

Perhaps I should grow old with grace,
I can't really keep up the pace,
There's nothing wrong with growing old,
We can still enjoy life, or so I'm told.

Vivien Shore

SUCH IS LIFE

I am writing this poem,
it's only penned for me,
I've got a lot of aches and pains,
Oh! My blooming knee.

A spinster and Great Aunt I am,
and now I'm over the hill,
my fingers have got cramp now,
wait! I need a pill.
I went to have my eyes done,
to see what he could find,
I couldn't even see the chart,
'*My dear*' you're nearly blind.

At night I take my glasses off,
my teeth they come out too,
it's just a sign of '*getting on*'
Oh wait! I need the loo.

I have a bed companion,
he really doesn't mind,
to see me looking such a fright
he really is quite kind.

I've shared my bed with him for years,
I know he'll always care,
He never laughs at me, you see -
He's just my Teddy Bear.

Anne McWiliams

A TOUCH OF GREEN EYE

I am being snubbed,
at the pop in parlour
to where I always go.

I have asked around a bit
but no-one wants to know

I have paid my tea money
and done my usual share.

But if I never went there again
I doubt that they would care.

It seems that since I've sat with Stan
a younger man of sixty four.

All my old mates don't want me around anymore,
I reckon it must be that I've pulled at seventy five.

No-one can be more surprised then I
I think he fell for my home-baked pie.

I don't want to sit in a corner just knitting socks
I want to cuddle up to Stan with a scotch on the rocks.

And when I go it will be with a smile
But I might pop back and haunt the parlour for a while.

Linda Fletcher

THREE SCORE

A magical groove that spells middle age
Your dumb days are over and now you're heralded as sage
The children are all now fully grown
And most of your seeds are allotted or sown
Your mortgage is now fully paid
And most of your future well laid
You may think slower but you know where you're at
You're in good shape and not even fat
Your raving days are over but you don't care
With your wife at your side you've lots to share
You'll never get bored for there's so much to do
And to your goals you've learnt to be true
You're nearing sixty but you don't feel old
You still possess vitality or so you're told
Discontent is a thing of the past
You've found your way and the dye is well cast
Now you have time to potter and think
And even research the missing link
The days chase each other and the months roll by
But you have not time to stand and sigh
There are places to go and new people to meet
And not just the ones you see in the street
With new doors to be opened and added to your list
For your life is not over. . . it's just time to discover the things you
        may have missed
Rejoice in the magical age that you've found
But take things steady and keep your feet on the ground
The struggles are over and the best lies ahead
With certainly no time to laze in your bed
The world is your oyster laid out for the ride
With all your life's skills being fully applied

Cherry Somers-Dowell

GROWING OLD

Look at me, look at me,
what do you see?
A child, a young woman,
a Mother of three?

A friend or a mistress
a Gran or a wife?
Look into my eyes
for a map of my life.

Look past the wrinkles,
the specs and the teeth.
Try hard to see
what's still there, underneath.

The casing is battered,
the inside is new.
Don't look away,
I'm a person, like you.

My thoughts, dreams and wishes
are treasures to find,
if you turn the key
to the vaults of my mind.

I'm a zombie, a hero,
a coward, all three,
but remember - I'm here,
I'm inside, I'm still *Me*

Jill Pickering

NIFTY SIXTY

Senior citizen, or OAP
Take your pick
They're the same to me.
We've planned for years
Just for this day,
No more slaving
We're off! Away!

To the sun, (watch my dust),
Get nice and brown,
Or is it rust?
We've done our duty,
Raised our kids,
So come on cutie
Let's hit the skids!

Linda Hudson

GRACEFUL OLD AGE

When young I envied old folk, their lives seemed very slow,
When pensioner then I thought, that's just, how mine will go,
Suddenly I'm sixty but I'm still out at work,
The years are speeding onward but nothing can I shirk.
At sixty six again a bride at last to me it seems,
I can retire and start to live the way I used to dream.
New husband's heart gave trouble, so once more into breach,
For he must take things easy if more years he's to reach,
I learn to run allotment, to clean our bungalow,
He has to take things steady, or out like candle blow,
Five years have sped so swiftly, I'm busy as a bee,
He plays upon his organ and teaches regularly,
I water our small garden go to the village shop,
Also write out poetry, have published quite a lot,
I've passed three score and ten years, and he's older than me,
But as for living graceful, no time for that you see,
I'm not quite sure what happened to gentle days I plan,
I know there's always something to do for me and man.
We're very, very happy our love would fill this page,
The only thing we cannot be, is graceful in old age.

Barbara Goode

SIXTY SOMETHING

I am sixty something
but also quite a bit more
and I wonder if you have guessed
anyway I am 'eighty four'.

I live in a bungalow here
'Number one' is its own name
and it is over sixty years
since my husband and I both came.

We have been so very happy
the people have been so kind
they have helped so many times
in all ways they could find.

My husband was very disabled
but is now in God's Kingdom of Heaven
and I am disabled as well
but God's grace to me is given.

And I am enabled to do
a work for Him right here below
to tell others of His wonderful love
and His love to the children to show.

As children all over the village
come to me for Bible reading and prayer
they come to me just any time
of the day or evening while I am here.

It gives wonderful joy to teach them
of the everlasting love of our God
revealed in Jesus our Saviour
through His glorious eternal word.

So even in my old age
tis so very true
this work for our God
makes my life ever new.

Doris Middleditch

EAGER ANTICIPATION

I'm fifty-two
And I'm telling you
I've really had more than enough
I've been working for years
And believe me, my dears
I can't wait till they pension me off!

Day after day and year after year
In the office I spend all my days
I quite often feel that I shouldn't be here
But the mortgage and food bills it pays

I don't mind admitting
That I'm not into knitting
But I'm sure I'll find something to do
The garden will take up a lot of my time
I might even start a new hobby too
'Cos my fingers are nimble and my mind is alert
I could even become a culinary expert

When I'm sixty something I'll have no apprehension
About retiring and claiming my well deserved pension

Angela Edwards

THE BIG 60

Sixty years, oh! What a drag
Wrinkles aching limbs!
I'm turning into quite a hag
I'm caught out for my sins

But wait a'mo, now I'm retired
I've time upon my hands
My bus pass I have just acquired
I'll visit foreign lands

Well anyway, I'll go to town
Or go to see my mates
No need to let things get me down
Now I go at pensioner's rates

There's half price tickets to a show
And also to the flicks
With reduced rates being so low
I'll go there just for kicks

My grandchildren come round to tea
I spoil them now, all three,
It isn't like they are my own
I hand them back, you see!

So being sixty's not so bad
When all is said and done
I haven't time to be sad
I'm having too much fun.

Edna Robinson

GETTING OLDER

'Silly old man,' my children say to me,
When I fought through the war, heroically!
They're trying to put me in a Home -
They've been to the bank to get a loan.

'Nice old man,' the nurses say to me,
When I've suffered their probings needlessly,
They're trying to put me in a grave -
There's too few beds; they need to save.

'Horrid old man!' The kids all shout at me,
When I tell them to be quiet, politely,
They're trying to smash my windows in,
They throw the milk bottles, steal the bin.

'Stupid old man,' the lawyers laugh,
The horrid chain-smokers who need a bath,
I only asked them 'Where's my Will?'
How was I to know I hadn't paid their bill?

'Poor old man,' my dead wife breathes,
She who listens, she who sees,
No-one else understands that I'm my own man:
And not just a sponger off the Pensioner's Plan.

Kathryn Gribble

AGE OF RETIREMENT

The age to retire is drawing near
Do you face it with gladness or fear
Lots are eager, and often say
I'll find lots to do each day
Hobbies, outings, a life of bliss
Now there'll be time to do all of this
So much can be done at leisure
Relaxation filled with pleasure
But what of those not wishing to retire
Only to work on, is their desire.
Maybe for those that is best
If they won't enjoy life's time of rest.

Merril Morgan

PASSED YEARS

Looking at my wristwatch
      The time was half past two
I went into the garden
      To see what I should do

Then I saw you standing there
      You came up to my side.
Placed your arm around me
      And asked me to be your bride

I thought I was just dreaming
      A dream that was so true
With all your love, you gave to me
      And all mine I gave to you.

Now my love the years have passed
      In the garden I'm not alone
I still see you standing there
      In the garden we called home

Audrey Cooper

SIXTY SOMETHING

When people look at me
What do they see?
Yes, I know my hair is grey,
White, some might say,
But my step is light
And I'm of good height;
Surely they could not be so bold
As to call me old!

On paper, I know, I'm sixty five,
A veritable OAP - snakes alive!
But behind the glasses and silver hair,
An ordinary guy, so don't you dare
Go labelling me, you ageist frump,
You know I'll only get the hump;
I know I've been around a while,
But going on in sterling style.

Truth to tell I know full well,
Within this maturer manly shell
There's the same me there'll ever be;
I'm not old, so hear my plea;
The memory may not be so good,
Nor run so fast as once I could,
But I refuse to give you quarter,
Just because you think I *'orter'*.

Time to do a bit of cookin'
Or just plain simple lookin',
Keeping fit in the local pool,
Working out and keeping cool;
Now to do a bit of gardening;
All must stop the arteries hardening;
Get on your bike; go for a hike,
These are the days you can really like.

Oh yes, I do get tired,
And retired, no longer hired,
A quick cat nap goes not amiss,
Well, in fact it can be bliss;
Now there's time for reading, writing,
But sport on tele can be inviting;
Value the space in this latter time;
One day, for me the bell will chime.

David Anderson

NIGHT THOUGHTS

When I go to bed at night
It's not to fall asleep,
But when one grows old
The night thoughts start to creep.

They are not the thoughts of children
Who dream of joyful days ahead,
Or of the love torn adolescent
Who let their hearts rule their head.

Oh yes I too had childhood hopes
Of sunny days and play,
Of poppy fields and buttercups
The smell of new mown hay.

And as an adolescent
I suffered the pangs of young love,
In my night thoughts there is one young man
Who picked up an expectantly dropped glove.

We would philosophise and dream of love
Thoughts as intense as oceans deep.
Then go to bed in tranquil mind,
Where night thoughts would not creep.

But without these sleepless nights of old age
The memories of the past will not be lost,
I can still walk through the poppy fields
Knowing they are not the haunting of a ghost.

Rita R Tabb

BIG SIX-O

Heinz 57 - three years tae go
Afore a hit - the big six-o
If truth be known - won't worry me
Fur I've been retired
Since I wis forty three!
Early retirement! That's whit
They call it noo
An' it basically means -
yer oan the buroo!
Fur - yer number's up
They want tae get rid
Oot - ye go - oan yer ear
Wi' jist a few quid
Noo - compensations - can be found
Although retired - I've no' gone underground
It's yer state o' mind!
Yon box - in yer heid
So keep oan wi' yer hobbies
An' yell no - go tae seed!

Irene Gunnion

RETIREMENT

How wonderful when we retire,
we'll laugh and dance all day.
There'll be no frantic rush to work,
We'll love and sing and play.

At 55 we'd looked ahead.
We'd worked so hard to be
so comfortable when we retired,
we felt we would be free.

At 60 - well the time was here.
We thought the work would end,
but chores continued - nothing changed.
We found we could not tend.

At 65 he too retired - he found that he was free
but what do you do with the time you have
when you can't walk or bend your knee?

By 70 your eyes have failed -
there are piles of books to read,
but the small print gradually grows feint,
and it's easy to sleep, you see.

At 75 the years rush by - there is so much to do
How can you sort the rubbish out, or throw away a screw?
Another five years gone and yet
80 seems far too soon to tidy up,
because it could be ten more years before we hit the gloom.

Doris Pullen

LOOKING BACK - GETTING OLD

Swiftly have the years rolled by.
Taking its toll of legs, ear and eye.
But bravely we face the coming years.
And try our best to calm our fears.

Youth, adolescence, marriage then birth.
All life's aspects have brought mirth.
But now as we gently grow older.
With wisdom we all look back behind our shoulder.

Experience we have gathered a plenty.
But to some we look now shattered and empty.
But although we may look of feeble frame.
Our years of learning has brought us far from shame.

Politicians have come and gone.
Whilst we have plodded on and on
The struggle for survival has always kept us going.
But now many see us as fit only for knitting and sewing.

Walking sticks and wheelchairs have become our symbol.
Ignoring the rest of use who are able.
However, we take all this in our stride.
For though we may be old, we have nothing to hide.

Able or disabled this is our final chapter.
Over the years we've seen both sorrow and laughter.
But in our final years of grace.
Let's pray pain and suffering does not take place.

David Whitworth

SIXTY SOMETHING

I was born in 'thirty two'
When Logie Baird perchanced to view,
The Derby at the Metropole,
While millions lingered on the dole.

Eight years have passed since lasted I toiled,
In hobbies now I am embroiled.
Now electronics are the rage,
My sort are called *'Stone Age'*

The humble thermionic valve glows red,
Now microchips are used instead.
My eyes are poor and hands are shaky,
Old fashioned parts suit me matey.

The hands of time speed faster now,
There's lots to do, but oh! My how.
Housework, gardens, shopping too,
I know, a *'purple heart'* will do.

My old cycle grinds away,
I need new legs before the day.
The Chinese move into Hong Kong,
And my pension comes along.

D Margerum

129

SIXTY - NOT OUT

Sixty is old! So youngsters say
But I don't feel old
I've just changed in a way,
No getting up early and going to work
I can just lie there oh! What a perk!
I have time to dream, and what's more!
Recall the years that have gone before.

I potter in the garden and lounge in the sun
Haven't a care about jobs to be done,
Holidays I've booked
There's so much to see
Places I've read about
Are calling to me.

My friends call round we just sit and chat
I've time to do puzzles and pastimes like that,
Books I love reading and do so at leisure,
And time with my grandson, I really do treasure.

No watching the clock, I've got all day
And just say *'Excuse me'* if I'm in your way
My pace maybe slower
But I'm not in a dream
My mind is quite active
My spirit is keen.

My life has a new meaning, I'm enjoying it too
With hobbies and leisure there's plenty to do,
New friends and new interests of a special kind
Sixty's not old! It's all in the mind.

Lilian France

INFORMATION

We hope you have enjoyed reading this book - and that you will continue to enjoy it in the coming years.

If you like reading and writing poetry drop us a line, or give us a call, and we'll send you a free information pack.

Write to

Anchor Books Information
1-2 Wainman Road
Woodston
Peterborough
PE2 7BU